MW01178579

LEGACY

Thirty Years of Haiku

LEGACY

Thirty Years of Haiku

WILLIAM SCOTT GALASSO

William Scott Galasso

Ⓖ GALWIN PRESS

Legacy: Thirty Years of Haiku
Published by GALWIN PRESS
LAGUNA WOODS, CALIFORNIA

Copyright ©2020 WILLIAM SCOTT GALASSO.
All rights reserved.

No part of this book may be reproduced in any form or by any
mechanical means, including information storage and retrieval
systems without permission in writing from the publisher/author,
except by a reviewer who may quote passages in a review.

All images, logos, quotes, and trademarks included in this book are
subject to use according to trademark and copyright laws of the
United States of America.

Library of Congress Control Number: 2020918172

GALASSO, WILLIAM SCOTT, Author
Legacy: Thirty Years of Haiku
WILLIAM SCOTT GALASSO

ISBN: 978-1-7327527-2-6

POETRY / Relationships/Family/Humor
POETRY / Haiku

QUANTITY PURCHASES: Schools, companies, professional groups,
clubs, and other organizations may qualify for special terms when
ordering quantities of this title. For information, email
galwinpress@yahoo.com.

All rights reserved by
WILLIAM SCOTT GALASSO and GALWIN PRESS.

This book is printed in the United States of America.

About the Author

William Scott Galasso is the author of sixteen books of poetry including Mixed Bag, (A Travelogue in Four Forms), 2018, and Rough Cut: Thirty Years of Senryu, 2019, available on Amazon. In 2017 he was co-editor/contributing poet of Eclipse Moon, the 20th Anniversary issue of SCHSG. His work has been published in more than 235 journals, anthologies and on-line publications in more than fifteen countries worldwide. In addition, he's participated in 300 readings and appeared on TV and radio programs in Washington, New York, New Mexico and California. His works include a Spoken Word audio CD - A Poet For All Seasons in 2009, and the following volumes of poetry:

- *Summer's Early Light,* in 1973.
- *Phoenix (Songs of the Firebird),* in 1981.
- *Emerald Rain* and *Cascadia,* (Haiku) in 1993.
- *Vermilion Falling,* (Haiku) in 1994.
- *Rainbow Music,* in 1995.
- *Cascade Cuneiform,* in partnership with (The Live Poets Society, a group Anthology), in 1995.
- *Full Moon Serenade,* (Haiku/Short poems) in 2001.
- *Blood (family) and Ink (Poems 1996-2003),* in 2003.
- *Odori, Blue, in 2004.*
- *Laughing Out Clouds, in 2007.*
- *PoetsWest CD - A Poet for All Seasons,* in 2009.
- *Sea, Mist and Sitka Spruce, (Poems 2007-2009).* A collection of (Haiku/Senryu/Tanka/Haibun/ Short Poems), in 2009.
- *Collage (Selected and New Poems), in* 2012.
- *Silver Salmon Runes, in* 2016.
- *Eclipse Moon,* Southern California, Haiku Study Group 20th Anniversary Issue contributing poet/editor, in 2017.
- *Mixed Bag: A Travelogue in Four Forms,* (Tanka, Haibun, Haiku Sequences, and short poems), in 2018.
- *Rough Cut: Thirty Years of Senryu,* in 2019.

Preface

I began writing about fifty years ago. In 1990, looking for a group of local writers to work with I responded to an ad written by Francine Porad, poet/painter/publisher and a leading light in the haiku community. She was at that time the moderator of Haiku Northwest and the publisher of Brussels Sprout. She became a mentor to me (and many others), over the years, introducing me to both the Japanese classicists and many other Haijin writers in English.

So, what is haiku? This is a question that has been debated and at times hotly disputed by various practitioners. Over the past fifty years the definitions of haiku have changed according to the Haiku Society of America several times. In 1976 haiku was defined as an unrhymed Japanese poetry recording the essence of a moment keenly perceived, in which nature is linked to human nature. It usually consists of seventeen onji (Japanese sound-syllables).

In 1993, HSA, adopted a new definition which though similar added imagistic language, to the definition. Charles Trumbull, editor of Modern Haiku expanded on previous definitions to speak about juxtaposition between two concrete images and alluded to a number of other values or rules one should follow to create a true haiku.

The statements in the paragraphs above, each make valid points and yet Harold Henderson an early haiku enthusiast and pioneer stated a true definition haiku is probably impossible and Dave Russo made the point that haiku has evolved from its traditional roots over the last 400 years, which can't be disputed. This fact was recognized and corroborated by the Matsuyama Declaration of September 1999 whose opening statement began as follows: *Haiku is part of world literature. Haiku is opening itself to various peoples of the world...* This short poetic form is now on the verge of broadening the possibilities of a rich array of poetic forms in the world.

The overall theme of the conference made a few essential points, one of them being an acknowledgment of the people and culture that created the form. But perhaps as important was recognition of diversity in cultures and the concept that each culture while respecting the spirit of haiku in Japan should develop its own expression and not merely imitate what was born in an early agrarian society.

To be sure we haiku enthusiasts share common ground upon which to build. One element agreed upon by all haiku poets is that haiku is a form known for its brevity.

Another element is recognition that at its root a connection exists between nature and human nature, despite the changes we ourselves have created. Examples are global warming and living in a more urban environment. In addition, we have created poetic off-shoots including monoku, sci-fi ku and others.

One may debate their quality and choose not to champion their cause, so be it, we are individual artists with our own values and sensibilities. We are not clones. That said, haiku enriches our lives by allowing us to see something in nature's essence and something in our own. It slows us down by encouraging our awareness, activates our senses, stimulates our intellect and sets free our spirits.

Finally, addressing a matter which I expect readers might have regarding a consistent pattern or viewpoint on any given subject. My answer is simple, we change, evolve, and are altered internally from one moment to the next. Further, we may feel more than one emotion at the same time; elated to have reached a destination, yet at the same time feel sorry a journey is over. Walt Whitman said it best, "Do I contradict myself, very well then I contradict myself, I am large, I contain multitudes." May you reader find in this work a journey worth taking.

NEW YEAR'S DAY

Happy New Year
in their eyes
an asterisk

yet another list
of New Year's resolutions
I'll never keep

New Year's Day...
she responds to the sound
of church bells

New Year's Day...
we speak with clouds
between us

New Year's Day
the couch conforming to
my well-fed bulk

New Year's Day...
hand in hand
our first resolution

New Year's Day...
meditation disturbed
...apple pie baking

New Year's Day...
under a frozen blanket
somebody's child

the year turns
her kiss on my lips
a little more urgent

WINTER

winter solstice
losing its last red leaf
crepe myrtle

peeling itself
from the frozen lake,
morning fog

scent of pine
careens through the house
clean taste of wind

clouds lift...
winter has come to
the mountains and me

under evergreens
silent as snowfall
night lingers

tramping uphill
hard rain softens
into snow

branches bare
yet snow frosted apples
cling to the tree

anticipating snow
horses huddle
against the wind

drifting snow
names on gravestones
disappear

a second falling
snow from the cedars
whitens my hat

snow melting
from still steaming
horse chestnuts

pale moon glow
caressing bare trees
and a sable sky

muddy footprints
cleaned by the falling
of crystalline snow

not the sky
but its stars falling
* * * snowflakes * * *

home wrecker
a hundred and eighty rings
on the Douglas fir

winter storm over
pecking at wild bird seed
native crows

the red cardinal
upsetting winter's clutch
invokes a shadow

bedridden wife...
all day our terrier
keeps her warm

working overtime
cat's tongue deep
in the eggnog

not even a dusting
just a few scattered flakes
fluttering singly

weathervane rooster
sits through storms
no fear of flying

wing over wing
tumbling in snow
cockeyed raven

cruel winter
I let the spider
keep his web

under mistletoe –
two friends awaken
to something deeper

roasting chestnuts...
that time of year again
in my native state

her finger in frost
tracing a heart...who is
this fortunate one?

snowflakes...
until the sea joins them
no two alike

winter darkness
what was left unspoken,
remains so

snowball fight
she aims
for my heart

indecision…
rain becomes snow
becomes rain

hearth fire crackles
your silhouette opens a door,
invites me in

aromatic foreplay
pervading the kitchen
wine moistened lips

shortest day
Christmas tree lights
in full bloom

winter wind—
we lean into
each other

longest minute...
counting the ring tones
before your voice

no caroling this year
where your voice was
now only the wind

becoming stream
the snowflakes
that fall into it

reaching into
my winter coat
winter wind

night music
the owl's minimalist
hoot-hoot

the carolers sing
expelling clouds
in perfect rhythm

homeless man
wearing Santa's hat
no toys in that bag

winter thaw
only the snowman's
pipe remains

incense smoke
melting window frost
Christmas morning

mistletoe,
her circuitous route
across the room

snow descends
at the pace of Satie's
Gymnopedie

star gazing
three kings
follow

Christmas Eve,
searching the night sky
for a certain star

in peace
star, cross and crescent
sharing the night sky

silent night, holy night
the train's long whistle
riding the plains

through the whiskey glass
the on and off blink
of Christmas lights

confronting crows—
a moonlit scarecrow's
silhouette on snow

Christmas day...
how bitter the snow
that keeps us apart

in places where
you never thought to see it
Christmas glitter

deepening
with each snowflake...
the silence

pier walk in Winter,
snowflakes and waves melting
into each other

paw prints in snow
blue chimney smoke
h o v e r s

ice
bending to earth
bare wires

little devils
lying in snow, waving arms
making angels

morning walk
the perfect pattern
of tires in snow

a storm of crows
beating down
the winter grass

outside the window
salvation an inch away
frozen sparrow

the last night
of a long year
paper cut

sun's last hurrah
purple mountains
pink snow

crows and gulls
in the same blue sky
not contending

rain streaked window
hunkered down crow
bares the weight of sky

taking down
the Christmas lights
her faraway eyes

Groundhog Day—
when does Punxsutawney Phil
not show his shadow?

tobogganing
parent and child
the same age

frost and fog...
the things I see clearly
the things I do not

Groundhog Day—
why so much depends on
the casting of shadows

off-season
horses without riders,
boardwalk carousel

snowball fight—
kids in their seventies
laughing out clouds

growing log by log
before the snowstorm
Dad's woodpile

winter sun seeps
through forest fog
...nothing is certain

black ice, sudden skid
recalling
all my yesterdays

my boots
her paw prints
side by side

loping from timberline
to mountain stream
the bear cub fisherman

sweet old dog
giving back to her
what she gives to me

laughing stone Buddha
on his neck a garland
of Mardi Gras beads

cougar tracks in snow
only now recalling
the lost kitten

racket at dawn...
black bear recycling
the garbage cans

boom of icebergs
calving into sea,
polar bear scatters

pug puppy...
wearing the worried look
of its owner

coffined snug
in a flower bed
old snow melting

cabin fever—
nothing between us
but my flannel shirt

snowy night
we spoon ourselves into
warmth, into sleep

on the tip
of my nose, soft scratch
of cat tongue

Presidents' Day
he thinks it is named
for himself

circuit breaker
not the only thing
tripping

snow on new buds...
the phone call
that never came

gasoline
on red embers
his words

where one a torch
was held on high
razor wire

raisins
in the porridge
...one moves

March first
following their own calendar
snow geese

tug-of-war
my socks, her socks
dog and I

stomping slush
from muddy boots
...the smell of stew

trouble ahead
trouble behind
...cracked ice

winter has come
to this body of mine
first stent

ice between us
not all of it
on snowy ground

ice circle
in the end you return
to yourself

Peeping Tom
at our window...I reach
for the cat snacks

Penitentes
between ice and fire
one step at a time

sipping black tea
on a gray afternoon
snow whitens the moor

beating down
the winter grass
a storm of crows

beside my shadow
ten feet tall, our dog's
cartoon silhouette

El Nino year
blooming in winter
the dogwoods

SPRING

Setsuban*
with each scattering of soybeans
prayers for good fortune

fair exchange
birdsong
for bird seed

defying old snow
shoots
of young grass

*Japanese celebration of the first day
of spring on the lunar calendar-Feb.

yellow-green moss
fleshing out ribs
of a fallen tree

snowmelt—
beaver dam swept
to the river's edge

Spring equinox
in an old peppertree
mockingbirds trill

lasting all day
yet frost melts
in a setting sun

silver in sunlight
icicles vanishing drop
by drop by drop

ice which held the stream
has become the stream
singing over stones

swollen creek
a bridge closed sign
someone ignored

snowmelt—
the spring releasing itself
from winter

streams arch
melts snow
steam rises

rain water running
down the icicle's sides
thinner, thinner...gone

snowmelt...
footprints left in
warming grass

erupting
from long sleep
birdsong

March, frigid rain...
finding every hole
in my wool sweater

moving day
I put out the last cupful
of birdseed

ibis and egret
sharing the stream
and minnows

moving day…
we empty the house
of ourselves

twenty-twenty
sign of the times
FOR SALE

pink snow on peaks
a lone fishing boat
cleaves the fogbank

in between
the old home and the new
this heart

not feeling joy...
I borrow the sound
of songbirds

armored with down
the strutting duckling
pipes and pecks

church bells...
one flock scatters
another prays

roadrunner antics
the monkey mind too
darts to and fro

tap dancing
on my leather hat
rain

Matinecock grave...
between two boulders
new leaves on the old oak

twisted metal
and a red beret
hard rain falling

Chinook wind
the words that came
unbidden

that levee
on the verge of breaking
my heart

flash flood
in the brown river
the red tent

between furrows
in the tulip fields,
ribbons of frost

yellow calendar
a red X on every page
but one

April arrives...
Painted Ladies swarm
in their millions

pruning grape vines
will she join me
when they ripen?

fox wedding weather
in each raindrop
a speck of sun

 Fire rainbow*
wild horses bend grass
beneath it

*The fire rainbow is the rarest naturally
occurring atmospheric event: clouds must be
cirrus, at least 20K in the air, contain just the
right amount of ice crystals and the sun must
hit the clouds at precisely 58 degrees.

above daffodils,
dragonflies hover
here   there

cherry blossoms...
not all that falls
this day

April, more poems
about cherry blossoms
than cherry blossoms

gnats and tax men
returning every April
...the rites of spring

saffron sunset
the metronome
of ventilators

Via Dolorosa
the good Samaritan
in mask and gloves

this sidewalk
too small for both of us
Covid-19

last goodbye
palm on glass
fingertips to lips

virus be damned
rabbits acting
like rabbits

dry cough
the question posed
in every mind

held high
a rainbow
of fists

past curfew
a cop and his son
kneel together

slapping cheeks
and cherry blossoms
hailstorm

cherry blossoms
the puppy sniffs
each fallen petal

hiding behind
cherry blossoms
full moon

cherry blossoms
how necessary, on this
grayest of gray days

Spring training
the new glove smells
of leather and oil

Spring training
she shows a rookie
the take sign

skylarking
the ball he never saw coming
falls at his feet

SMACK...a homer
the heckler's mouth
snaps shut

Sunday baseball game
she throws me
another curve

sun shower
married this day
twenty years

bent rim, torn net
no "plunk", no "swish"
on the old court

morning quake
the solid ground
not so solid

spring garden,
among several stone frogs
an impostor leaps

twilight
the red fox enters
the garden

Green tea
in our green garden
first bumblebee

frowning gardener,
among the purple lilacs
cigarette butts

swallow's arabesque
her circuitous logic
makes me dizzy

despite lymphoma
the jacaranda's petals
entice our little dog

mountains
through my window
melting in the rain

torrential rain...
her estranged brother's
sudden death

rows and rows of cars
parallel parking near
rows and rows of tulips

sun shower over—
carried on a wind gust
the scent of lilacs

two stories up
cat on the windowsill
sunning herself

vanishing into
size twelve boots
the kittens head

riding
water bed waves
bored cat

largesse
the rush of koi
to my hand

for the first time
I meet a northwest native
...aplondontia

on their skins
the cows share
day and night

coyote howls
kids and cats
take flight

Sunday brunch
morning glories open
over jasmine tea

shaft of light
spearing the forest
traps a grazing doe

on promenade,
a boxer named Buttercup
walks her owner

Boston terrier
still swathed in
its puppy smell

chasing swallows,
the puppy's
perfect somersault

my dog's black nose
finds the bee hidden
in pink camellia's

over rain's hum
and the stream's gossip
a wet dog yelps

tears in her eyes,
first walk in the park
without our dog

half-moon over
Half Moon Bay, a dolphin
leaps to its light

millipede...
a thousand legs, yet
you tread so softly

woodpecker beating
a distant tattoo,
roommate wanted

falcon at rest
his sharp eyes
never leave us

bobbing
among the tombstones
rooster

Churchill Downs
a parade of horses
and lady's hats

April showers—
the cursive flow
of pen on paper

edge of sleep
a carillon's bells
cross the lake

her lipstick
and the tulips
same haughty red

discovering—
the hole in my shoe
forsythia bud

renewal of faith
...the swallows return
to Capistrano

the old deck gone
new coat of paint
our own home
...becoming

tinkle of wind chimes...
is that the sound of the dead
passing among us?

field of lavender
bees hum and two
become one

cat's yammer
chickadee's canto
their duet...not in sync

white puffs of cloud
every cottonwood tree
seeding sky

temple ruins—
morning mist just
passing through

after rain—
so sweet the air, I fill
my lungs with it

in the lurch of its leap
     tree frog
bends bamboo leaves

May flurries…
a spider web snares
the cottonwood seeds

hard rain
locked door
no key

Irish setter
the perfect metronome,
of its wagging tail

bamboo flute…
mallards paddle toward
the sound

crowning
Paprika yarrow
Monarch butterfly

Matilija poppies...
a craving for eggs
sunny side up

red balloon
a child's eyes,
ascend into sky

Chichen Itza
faces in flesh and stone
nearly identical

first date...
the parrot with his voice
makes a pass

in the same lagoon
where tourists swim,
natives feed crocodiles

spring garden
from the old volunteer
new shoots

red licorice
the child's frown morphs
into a smile

playground roar
by the sound of it
a homer

avian madrigal
in dappled woods
I just tweet

a hummingbird
siphons the sugar water
...whir of wings

streetlamps on...
nightingale's nocturne
begins

fog over sea
sunrise
lifts it up

praying mantis
the little girl's hands
come together

ten in the morning
a half moon
fades into blue

thread by thread
circles entrap both
fly and spider

ladybug
traversing my arm
all eyes on me

dragonfly
on the turtle's back
smear of moss

slow migration
two feet of concrete
banana slug

cloister garden
stained glass wings
of a dragonfly

sweet air...
is that your spirit
passing on the breeze?

encircling
the wishing well
wildflowers

sea breeze...
the salt inside me
answers

chemotherapy
a mile-long strip
of roadside poppies

thirteen cranes
the city skyline
readjusts

rainbow then only the rain

needle in the arm
just a test
for now

Flag Day
some upside down
this year

SUMMER

can't sit still
last day of school
dog and butterfly

Summer solstice...
the longest day begun
an otter swims alone

June garden
speaking of dragonflies
...one appears

in her sun hat
gardening, she hums
our song

in mid-air
by the koi pond...
kitten's paw

cloudless sky,
the Ferris Wheel turns
into summer

art patrons
drawn to the fair
cooking smells

small town festival
a bearded lady greets
saucer-eyed children

he tugs her arm...
cherry shaved ice
bleeds into sand

mid-morning
guiding the trawler
pilot whale

Summer breeze
cattails whisper where
water meets land

trisected
by tall reeds,
blue heron

neap tide
the languid stride of
a Blue Heron

water striders
skimming the koi pond
...one disappears

cruise ship
fewer hands waving
this year

warm summer night
he serenades the goldfish
with his bamboo flute

midday heat...
the buzz of cicadas,
splitting air

desert winds,
tumbleweeds encircle
the old corral

raspberries
maybe their taste
will sweeten her words

mirage...
a pillar of fire rising
from the Salton Sea

blistering heat
dust devils
swirl maniacally

after the fire...
smell of scorched earth
and pepper tress

fireweed
where the cabin stood,
rebuild or let be?

staccato grunts
escape the arroyo,
javelina in lust

firestorm
stolen memories,
swollen eyes

three still crows
anchored on church steeple
sunbathing

summer heat
angry young men
ambulance songs

full daylight
barn owl beached
...firestorm

her tone of voice...
one hundred degrees
in the shade

Ephesus
the brothel's location
carved in marble

the Amalfi drive
on a cliff climbing bus
"Hail Mary, full of grace"

born here, she said
never left the Rock
three square miles

* Rock of Gibraltar

bumblebee
bending to earth
dandelion

early morning
just crickets and the one
who listens to them

choosing
the same plum
yellow jacket and I

worker ant
the breadcrumb
twice his size

sunburnt skin,
now purple where
the spider bit me

extinguished by
a chainsaw's whine,
cicadas buzz

feet in wet sand
passing pelicans
skim the waves

fish tossing
the market tourists
click in tune

fisherman's net
heavy with its catch
  of plastic

something enigmatic
about the dolphin's smile
marine Mona Lisa

driftwood
how many waves,
how many years

splitting fog—
in the pelican's bill
a flapping fish

jellyfish and seaweed
new scents excite
the old dog's nose

Neptune's visage
sea whittled driftwood
a million waves

boogie boarding:
my wife and
her inner child

sea born mist—
softening cedars
into themselves

little hands reach
for the koi, big hands
for the toddler

still lake
the moon reinvents
itself

Indian River...
pink flamingoes on
tailored lawns

as if that summer
long ago never ended
buzz of cicadas

hot summer's day
through the shoji screen
bathers' silhouette

summer squall—
through rain streaked glasses
the orange jersey

braving the red flag
of undertow, breathless
I lie on white sand

under placid water
of the silent pond
snapping turtle

thunderclap—
ending the couple's
sullen silence

heat lightning
exposing the river bend
deep in the canyon

soon to be paper
green as a dollar bill
cedar stand

snail on stucco
the long, slow climb
into light

afterglow
the eagle's glide
in silhouette

Snoqualmie Falls—
her long hair jeweled
with rising mist

sunrise tai chi
footprints erased
in the chant of waves

midsummer night
my toes, your heels
mold sand

lights across the bay,
is someone over there
looking over here?

tea rose dawn
bare feet laved by
the cool Pacific

rolling sea
waves swallow
the risen moon

ankle deep in sand
feeling the pull of
an outgoing tide

stargazing
the caress of waves
on bare feet

beyond waves rising
from the asphalt's mirage
Pacific breakers

seaweed grazing...
the one-legged gull
discovers a mussel

sand dunes
the sounds of a couple,
coupling

stone fence—
fossils tell stories
of a bygone sea

hard rain falling
and with it the sound
of sizzling steaks

an old farmer
waves with his pipe,
Pocono summer

scent of hay,
swept away by
summer rain

NORTH*
ABOVE
me in the middle
GORGE BELOW

Summer breeze,
as llamas graze
fur flutters

distant mowers hum
warm winds rifle trees
buzz of cicadas

bar-be-que
and new mown grass
summer scents

rising heat
a multitude of peppers
all shapes, all sizes

too damned hot...
walk in my shadow
just this once

the saddle cradles
my head, sickle moon
in a sable sky

round bellied
mare on the ranch
eating for two

box canyon—
the sandstone echoes
of horses running

finding their stride
colts embroider the pasture
with unshod hooves

summer heat
her palms smell
of horse sweat

synchronized
mare and colt
nibbling, nuzzling

cricket be quiet,
it's after midnight and
I need my sleep

dodging raindrops,
the mosquito targets
a sleeping dogs' ears

a muffled buzz...
the fat fly careening
in cupped hands

circling above
a cloud-filled lake,
seven bald eagles

swift glide
a hawk's shadow
cuts mine in two

gin and tonic, July
the slight dissipation
of tropical heat

crowded bistro
only the bartender
knows I exist

Fourth of July
the bombast
of politicians

Independence Day
a man carries a sign
"will work for food"

barefoot
the sand gives,
just enough

4th of July
our celebration
smells of Sulphur

smudge of fog
in the cave, in the cove
surf break echoes

beach combing
just broken shells,
plovers and me

sun shower—
sweeping the gulls from
their dockside roost

gnarled hands on
soft hands, the how-to
of hooking worms

rogue wave
...curling me back
into myself

scratched heart
in beach sand, only
the names change

storm tossed beach...
amidst flotsam and jetsam
a rusting harpoon

passing schooner
sails in silhouette
shading the sun

summer shower
ever so slightly
her ardor cools

lunar halo
its radiance encircles
the chapel's cross

Summer night—
a voice at my back
not heard in years

feet in sand
something pulls me
towards deeper water

deep indigo
the cratered moon
full of itself

shard of the moon
cuts obsidian sky
a lone owl hoots

no moon tonight
only the Milky Way
and fireflies

hanging
from a cloud
sickle moon

jackhammers...
building a road
between us

all day laboring
spiders work undone
sweep of a cat's paw

pastel pink
and powder blue sky
Confirmation Day

scarlet begonias
dressing an old house
in sultry hues

playing peekaboo
with hips and shorts
her turtle tattoos

marked with henna
her hands present
a white lotus

mountain peaks
in the sundog's aura
her silhouette

Summer moon
coyotes do what
coyotes do

sundog
turkey buzzard circles
in its aura

Sierra switchbacks
she loves me not,
she loves me

potter's field
nameless bones teaching
forgotten things

Light Pillars…
the shadows cast between
earth and sky

Lenticular cloud
on the king of mountains
a crown

across
the mountain's face
cloud shadows crawl

wilderness calls...
I lose the trail
to find myself

roadside cross
...fresh roses
absent friends

pacing the ferry
a lone gull
wings north

low tide...
all that lay hidden
brought to light

dead whale
one less song is heard
in the sea

turquoise sea
cobalt sky
the usual clouds

Blue Hole
how deep we plunge
to find...

another ocean
same rhythm
in breaking waves

mussel squirt
the puppy's paws
rake sand

tasting sea salt
on your tongue
...gulls sweep the sky

after rain
sweeps the air
sea scent

storm driven gulls
side by side with crows
in the greening corn

seaside boardwalk—
splinters can't stop
her barefoot dancing

cacophony
from the rookery
screeching gulls

sunflowers
the way I'll always
remember her

trapped inside...
a flyswatter used to free
the honey bee

dragonfly
the sun through wings
of stained glass

between letters
and marbled rosettes,
headstone moss

thunder clap...
the puppy
barks back

coming home
the pogo bounce
of my dog

entering
the puppy's ear
child's lullaby

largest flower*
twice in a lifetime
this wonder

*Amorphophallus titanium (cadaverous flower)
75 kilos, blooms 3 days every 40 years in
Veracruz

rumble of thunder—
spokes on a bicycle
begin to blur

thunderstorm
all that anger
put to flight

bleeding mist
mountains after
the summer storm

emerging from
the muddy stream
teetering horse

clouds droop
mist rises
we make love
in shades of gray

belly of a horse,
for grazing chickadees
a wide umbrella

rose sand...
the diamondback leaves
its squiggly S

train whistle
sweeping the pass
coyote's howl

dusk
ambling in silent pastures
horse silhouettes

in the drought year
"Brown is beautiful"
proclaims a sign

dog days
after the argument
separate trains

parched...
in her kiss

sweet summer rain

August heat wave
her pregnancy,
unplanned

from burnt rubble
of blackened stumps
only fireweed stands

five-year drought...
our child at the window
mesmerized by rain

big kids swing
I throw my legs
into sky

sunset...
above a ribbon of fire
first evening star

tumbleweeds
the wooden cross
without a name

hunting hawk
the sniper
adjusts his sight

baby's trauma
a warehouse full
of elephant tusks

crossing the trail...
a baby diamondback
rattles its warning

fog burning off
a bask of crocodiles
by the riverside

the soundtrack
of summer lust...
bullfrog's basso

on our love seat...
a stub tailed lizard
practices push-ups

sunset...
beneath magenta clouds
the sea on fire

moonrise
the dog's ears stand
when coyotes sing

full moon
night-blooming jasmine
spurs a memory

Labor Day,
the first geese
heading South

sleeping in rags
on a cardboard box
another statistic

post 9/11
passing over...
the first jet

wearing old/
new clothes
new/old man

on the T.V. news
scarecrows
fighting for rice

the crisscross
of ferryboats
oh, what a night

day moon
it's perfect circle
fades into blue

jacaranda
bougainvillea,
her saffron sari

selling our house
how bittersweet
our cherries taste

September morning
an apple for the mare
her muzzle's softness

bottle with barnacles
no message inside...
just current events

hiss of sea on sand
the words she whispers
in my ears

amidst apple pulp,
the sugar buzz
of yellow jackets

summer's end
passing the hearse
while I still can

small town America
the last drive-in movie
shuts down
  summer's end

cusp of autumn
a fisher feast of salmon
in the birthing stream

AUTUMN

Autumn equinox
a pebble pings
the windshield

stars above
mist at my feet
heading for work

meteor shower
so many wishes
falling to earth

shooting star...
even the heavens seem
restless tonight

mudslide—
a little girl clings
to her comfort bear

last steps of portage
boats find water again
hands remember oars

yellow school bus
in its wake
autumn leaves

sunning himself
in the autumn air,
three-legged cat

stepping on
each sidewalk crack,
cross-eyed cat

fish ladder climb
the irresistible urge
of spawning salmon

Salmon Day's Fest—
more people this year
than spawning fish

life and death marry
in the mountain stream
spawning salmon

dawn
salmon cirrus clouds,
a sliver of moon

my friend's smile
perched on a salmon
he caught

seaside café
out of season,
lukewarm chowder

resting my axe
for spiced cider,
blackberry pie

cutting firewood
already warming
to the task

squirrel's chatter
as I hone my ax, not
their nuts I'm after

orchard fresh
sweet apple...
bitter worm

their stump gone
cats rolling in
the wood chips

icebreaker
on the haiku path
wild berries

chopping wood…
blue tint of smoke near
the moonshiner's still

exploring the woods
a boy finds an arrowhead
the deer too are gone

picking
the last ripe plum
autumn wind

"It's so big!"
She squeezes me,
harvest moon

bronze plaque
this sycamore older than
the country it lives in

on the outside
as it is on the inside
rain

windstorm over
strand by strand
the spider rebuilds

Tor in the mist...
first the whistle
then the falcon

corn moon
over ripening fields
the baby in her belly stirs

windblown
leaves
shadowbox

no harvest more sweet
from our own orchard...
apples and pears

Harvest moon
our next door neighbor
...gone

emerging
from green jacket
yellow corn

losing her sight, Granny
waves at the scarecrow
in our neighbor's field

white corn harvest
the truck's sweet cargo
soon to meet my teeth

128

sunset—
buck and doe
in silhouette

harvest time—
deer culling
the apple trees

cabin porch
the sound of moss
in valley fog

nandin berries
the color her cheeks
take on

road kill
the sadness
of deer eyes

freeway jam
a harvest moon mellows
our need for speed

terminal...
still the gardener
plants his bulbs

Giant's Causeway—
is it mist or myth
that enraptures here?

wearing wrinkles
on their wrinkles
Shar pei puppies

dogs run free
contributions
to the compost pile

she curls
around the dog, I
around them both

season over
the stadium's silence
seeps into me

against the tide
tug towing barge
back to the want ads

laid off...
red leaves fill
the gutter

job hunting...
unclaimed pumpkins
in the compost pile

ghost pines...
the dreams I
left behind

another birthday
the leaves fall more
swiftly now

whack of a hammer
the town becoming
a ghost of itself

hard rain...
the street noise
grows louder

autumn storm
among the flotsam
a robin's nest

window gazing
on a crisp autumn day
...the grouch is gone

busker's tune
a rasp of leaves down
the cobblestone mews

shapes shifting
a starling murmuration*...
some lead, some follow

*what a "flock" of starlings is called

shafts of light
spearing the forest
trap a grazing doe

Indian summer,
wrens add their songs
to the gypsy wind

sunset
fire in the sky, the leaves
...your eyes

frost on cattails
a mallard in the slough
swims alone

disappearing
reappearing
jo er   the
 gg   in   mist

every muscle
in my leg, feeling this
mountain I climb

young legs retrieve
what old legs cannot
windblown hat

softening the stone
of castle walls,
morning mist

wild geese…
my only suitcase
packed and ready

even the caged bird fall migration

passing swiftly
in the sky above, the sound
of one goose honking

border crossing
no passport, no visa
...wild geese

triad of geese...
just wings and the will
to use them

geese before me,
cars behind me
all honking

freight train
its length measures
the valley

clear cut
the mountain slipping
into mountain streams

tramping uphill,
hard driving rain
softens into snow

food bank...
the pear from my tree
elicits a smile

windswept away
frozen footsteps
mapping my path

stadium empty
but if you listen
very closely...

coming home...
on muddy boots
foreign soil

daybreak
in the rear-view mirror
retirement home

frost on cattails
a mallard
swims alone

deep frost
not in our garden
alone

between lake fog
and cumulus clouds
mountain peaks

hill climb,
headlights tracing
switchbacks

faceless no longer,
the pumpkin glaring
with fire in its eyes

fog and chimney smoke
the road less traveled
now barely seen

more grotesque
than their smiles
smashed pumpkins

row of sugar pumpkins—
awaiting the carvers' knife
and brand new faces

Halloween party—
dancing with Shakespeare
Medusa

pumpkin patch, this
year the scarecrow wears
Uncle Sam's hat

Halloween night
candy eating zombies
take over the hood

black and orange
koi fish in a pond
dressed for Halloween

somber sky
the crow flaps wings
just once

wind gust...
with each leaf fall
more sky

bouncy bridge
the cautious crossing
of retirees

rasping leaves,
milky cataracts
in the old dog's eyes

leaf peepers gaze
at passing geese, a feather
floats among them

I am burning leaves
along with bridges of youth
...the old love letters

letting go
this life,
autumn leaves

brown leaves
rasping on pavement...
don't look back

beside me
the patter of paws
on maple leaves

old truck, maple leaf
in the door handle
hitching a ride

our feet swish,
swish swimming
through fallen leaves

early October
treetops dripping
maple leaves

untethered by wind
vermilion leaves pirouette
the cat's whirling eye

yellow school bus
harvesting children
the valley   quiet

after much practice
a child's stuttered scrawl
becoming his own name

family reunion
hurricane warnings
dominate the news

shrieking children
putting my pen down
the curse...unspoken

repeating words
big brother spoke, I visit
the principal's office

hurricane season
wind and rain lash
our denial

tsunami
as the word is spoken
it arrives

November morning
solitary wasp tapping
on frosted windows

hitchhiker gives thanks
for the lift, offers
a gift of mushrooms

tsunami...
in the wreckage, a doll
without its child

mushroom gathering
smells of wet earth
fill the stock pot

leaves which once
provided shade crunch
beneath my heels

turkeys fattening
the woodsman honing his axe
Thanksgiving coming

frost on the roof
fog on the lake
the joy of spooning

giving thanks
for our chosen family,
glasses clink

Thanksgiving prayer
already answered,
she sleeps beside me

Thanksgiving Day...
one pink rose
lingers on the bush

test results
come back negative
...Thanksgiving

Thanksgiving over...
crowds fill malls, to gorge
on holiday gifts

days grow short
snow creeps
down the mountain

cedar branches
turning the color of rust
Autumn or acid rain

under my feet
a thousand years
of leaf fall

December first
feral kitten seeks adoption
...come on in

last day of autumn
in the firelit doorway
her silhouette

Acknowledgments

The author wishes to thank the editors and publishers of the following for choosing these poems which appeared in the in the following journals, anthologies, and on-line publications:

HNW & HSA Anthologies: When Butterflies Come 1993, an HSA members Anthology as are 1995 Sudden Shower, Echoes Across the Cascades, 1996 Unbroken Curve, 1997 Sunlight Through Rain, 1998 Cherry Blossom Rain, 1999, The Swinging Grasshopper, 2000 To Find the Words, Wind Five-Folded (Tanka Anthology, AHA Books), All Day Long (HPNC Anthology), Geese (Anthology) 1999, HSA Anthology 2000 Crinkled Sunshine, Wind Shows Itself (Haiku NW), 2004, Tracing the Fern (Haiku North America anthology), 2005, HSA anthology Loose Change 2005, Lanterns: a Firefly Anthology 2007, Among Water Lilies, A White Lotus Anthology 2008, Seed Packets: an anthology of flower haiku, 2009, a Bottle Rockets anthology, Sharing the Sun, 2010 HSA anthology, In Pine Shade, 2011 HSA members anthology, HNA Standing Still a 2011 Anthology, Dreams Wander On: Contemporary Poems of Death Awareness, ed. Robert Epstein (a 2011 Anthology), The Temple Bell Stops: Contemporary Poems on Grief, Loss and Change, by Robert Epstein (a 2012 anthology), This World, (a 2013 HSA Anthology), Now This: Contemporary Poems of Beginnings, Renewals, and Firsts (a 2013 Anthology); A Warm Welcome (a 2013 Seabeck anthology); No Longer Strangers, (a 2014 Haiku Northwest Anthology); Take Out Window, HSA 2014 anthology. The Spirit in Contemporary Haiku, ed. by Robert Epstein 2014, Rainsong, (a 2014 Seabeck anthology); Drawn to the Light, SOCAL Anthology, 2015, A Splash on Water, HSA 2015 anthology. Fire in the Treetops (Celebrating Twenty-five Years of Haiku North America), 2016 HSA anthology What the Wind Can't Touch, Every Chicken, Cow, Fish and Frog (Animal Rights

Issue), 2016 Write Like Issa How-to Anthology),
2017. 2017 HAIKU CANADA REVIEW, Eclipse
Moon, 2017 SoCal 20th Anniversary Issue,
Earthsigns HNA 2017 Anthology, On Down the
Road, HSA 2017 Anthology, Haiku Canada A Far
Galaxy 2018, Gift of Silence: A Haiku Tribute to
Leonard Cohen, HSA 2020 members Anthology
Four Hundred and Two Snails, All the Way Home:
Haiku on Aging, ed. Robert Epstein, 2019, British
Haiku Society Anthology, A Train Haiku
Anthology, 2019. Lummox 8, A Moment's Longing
SCHSG, HSA Nick Virgilio Haiku Association 2019
Anthology, Vol. 1 BHS Anthology: Root 2019.
SCHSG 2020 Anthology A Sonic Boom of Stars,
Smoke from My Candle (Haiku Canada).
Haiku/Senryu (journals and magazines) : Cicada,
Red Pagoda, Modern Haiku, Brussels Sprout,
Mirrors, Backyard Bamboo, Woodnotes, Tandava,
Antfarm, Haiku Headlines, Frogpond, New Cicada
(Japan), Lynx, Haiku Canada, New Zealand Haiku,
Ko (Japan), Piedmont Literary Review, black
bough, San Francisco Haiku Anthology, Bear
Creek Review, Northwest Literary Forum, Point
Judith Light, Haiku Northwest booklet '93, HWUP,
Tight, Blithe Spirit (Essex, England), Lilliput
Review, Albatross (Romania), Haiku Haven,
Orphic Lute, Wheel of Dharma, Honolulu
Advertiser, Spin (New Zealand). Ant, ant, ant,
ant, ant, VRABAC (Sparrow) (Croatia), Haiku
Quarterly (England), Hummingbird, Raw Nervz
(Canada), Seaoats International, Haiku Presence
(England), Tundra, Chiyo-Laughing CyPress,
Silver Wings, Hokumeisha Haikukai (Japan),
Paper Wasp (Australia), Heron's Nest. A Hundred
Gourds (Australia). Key-ku: Haiku of the Keys
(Solares Hill), Brevities, Treetops, Famous
Reporter (Australia), Mariposa, White Lotus,
Blackwidow's Web of Poetry, Haiku Hippodrome,
Moonset, South by Southeast, HAIKU PAGE,
Wisteria, Kokako (NZ), California Quarterly,
seashores (Ireland).

Online journals/Blogs- Simply Haiku (Senryu section), electronic magazine, Asian Geographic Magazine (the Read), (Singapore), Cattails, (Haiku Oregon), Four and Twenty Kernels, Sonic Boom (India), Frozen Butterfly (Austria) Prune Juice, Autumn Moon Haiku Journal, Under the Basho (India), The Bamboo Hut, Otata (AU), Stardust.

Reviews of Previous Books

Summer's Early Light (1973)
Phoenix (Songs of the Firebird) (1981)
Cascadia and Emerald Rain (1993)
Vermilion Falling (1994)
Cascade Cunieform (1994)
(Sold Out)
Haiku/Senryu Collections

Mini-Reviews
Full Moon Serenade (2001)

Galasso's sense perceptions are vibrating with song... this book of poetry is a gift to the reader.

> tasting sea salt
> on your tongue
> & gulls sweep the sky

Marjorie Buettner, Modern Haiku

Odori, Blue (2004)

His poems are crisp, and honest, written with a deft touch that is uniquely beautiful.

Carrie Anne Thunell, White Lotus/Nisqually Delta Review

Laughing Out Clouds (2007)

There is a sense of yugen (or mystery) in many of these poems. It is a mystery that inspires us to slow down visualize nature and breathe poetry—Galasso's poetry.

Marjorie Buettner, Book Editor, Moonset

I'll never forget reading this collection...beautiful, insightful and uplifting poetry resonates with any reader with a soul.

Paul Rance, Editor, Peace and Freedom Press

Sea, Mist and Sitka Spruce (Poems 2007-2009)

Another collection by the very prolific William Scott Galasso... in a wide selection of haiku and mainstream journals... I particularly enjoyed the autumn and winter images...

Moira Richards, Book Editor, Moonset, South Africa

Silver Salmon Runes (2016)

I get a sense of authenticity and integrity as if I were reading someone's journal.

Randy Brooks, Frogpond

Keen observations that do what good haiku do: provide a unique viewpoint on the ordinary world.

Marjorie Buettner, Modern Haiku

Mixed Bag: A Travelogue in Four Forms (2018)

Galasso is a talented and unique writer. Mixed Bag is a good book of poetry that takes us through Galasso's many travels, experiences, and philosophies. Galasso effectively makes use of haibun, haiku sequences, short free verse poems, and tanka to showcase his world of adventure.

Dave Read, Haiku Canada

This "legacy series" of poems, culled from previous book and publications is indeed, a mixed bag. Galasso combines free verse, haiku, haiku sequences, haibun and tanka with a mélange of travel destinations geographical and emotional. Plenty of haibun and haiku stick in the mind like postcards worthy of a prominent place on a corkboard or refrigerator door. Yet though we travel the world, someplace in the heart remain mutely mysterious, *nothing to say/only my hands and arms/can speak.*

Editors, Modern Haiku

Rough Cut: Thirty Years of Senryu (2019)

Rough Cut: Thirty Years of Senryu by William Scott Galasso has an introduction where clarification of the title is given: suggesting "that as human beings we are but works in progress, intellectually, emotionally and spiritually. My hope is that you may recognize your own dramatis personae among the senryu you find here or that you may connect with those you've touched or been touched by on this life's journey."

It is safe to say that in thirty years most people experience an amazing range of experiences and William Scott Galasso has certainly lived a very full, eclectic and keenly observed life that he has documented faithfully and poignantly in Rough Cut. There is a wealth of living and a rewarding spectrum of life that Scott has presented in this collection with a perspicacious poise, passion and purpose. The human condition is illuminated throughout in this no holds barred collection that is noteworthy for its candor and directness.

While Rough Cut states that it is "Thirty Years of Senryu" I found much more than just senryu in these pages. As I first began reading this epic sequence I actually wondered if the amount of senryu, over 300, might desensitize me if I read too many at once. It didn't. What I discovered is that beside memorable senryu zingers there are little poems, some haiku, some gentle life sketches and some lovely and intimate tributes to family members and lovers, with details that transcend the personal and touch on universal situations and experiences. The variety in tone, subject matter and the quality throughout makes this a distinguished and extensive collection.

> child asleep
> daddy still reading
> Prince Caspian

home movies
the living and the dead
at play again

I'll miss the lark song
in the morning she said...
then closed her eyes

There are equally powerful poems about strangers caught in
the flotsam/jetsam of life on the edge and heart of woe that
reminds of the gravity that claims people in every walk of
life.

bitter wind
on a bus station bench
anonymous

bottle
broken as the life
beside it

after a meal,
shower and shave, the hobo
who looks like us

This is a collection with such breadth and depth that it is
difficult to summarize, but I am sure everyone will recognize
themselves or their friends and their family somewhere in
these pages. It is a book I highly recommend.

Reviewed by Tom Clausen

In Rough Cut, one finds numerous poems addressing human
foibles that do include kigo:

my father's anger
approaching the purple
of ripened plums

This poem shows another permission of senryu: the use of
schemes and tropes, in this case a simile. Here are two
more, the first with a seasonal reference, the second without

pg. 39. Both show the sort of word play usually discouraged
in haiku.

> she zigs
> he zags
> mating season

> separated
> by a common language
> his and hers

Galasso has engaged with many topics in his thirty years of
exploring the human experience, from family relationships to
social commentary, through war, dying and death, to label
but a few. Here are some I found quite affecting.

> widower
> through a window
> pixilated by rain

> border town
> neighborhood children play
> red light, green light

> the bass hum
> of bow on strings...
> her deepest secret

Galasso concludes his Introduction with the hope, "that you
may recognize your own dramatis personae among the
senryu you find here or that you may connect with those you
have touched or been touched or been touched by on this
life's journey." I have recognized. I have connected.

Maxianne Berger, Haiku Canada

Special Acknowledgments

I wish to thank talented doctor, writer, poet and archivist Bruce Feingold for taking the time in his busy schedule to read this book (more than once). I appreciate the thoughtful commentary he provided which appears on the back cover of this collection and am grateful for his willingness to take on the work. In gratitude, I would like to provide this bio for Bruce immediately below:

Bruce H. Feingold is a practicing Bay Area psychologist, an award-winning poet and author of A New Moon, old enough, Sunrise on the Lodge and arrhythmia. He is on the Board of Directors of The Haiku Foundation, Chairman of the Touchstone Awards, and vice president of the Haiku Poets of Northern California.

In addition, I would also like to thank my wife Vicki for her support of my work, technical assistance and inspiration. Susie Schaefer of Finish the Book Publishing for her editorial and technical expertise and artist Deanna Estes of Lotus Design for her fine cover design work. Your contributions to this work were invaluable and are much appreciated.

Photographs

All photos used in this book are by the author except the back cover photo by Vicki Galasso.

Cover: Split, Croatia
New Year's: Seattle, WA
Winter: Seattle, WA
Spring: Fullerton, CA
Summer: Lecce, Italy
Autumn: Seattle, WA

Made in the USA
Columbia, SC
27 October 2020

23499304R00093